William G. Davies Jr.

Before There Were Bones

Before There Were Bones

William G. Davies Jr.

Prolific Press Inc.

Acknowledgements:

The Cortland Review; "The House" The Wilderness House
Literary Review; "A Place In The Shade" The Wilderness
House Literary Review; " TKO" Jellyfish Whispers; "A
Wynken, Blynken and Nod Moment" Foliate Literary
Magazine; "Along the Road" Everyday Poets; "Art"
Wilderness House Literary Review; "Ash Wednesday"
Wilderness House Literary Review; "Kittyhawk" Bluepepper;
"Kissed by God and Ski Roundtop" Bluepepper; "Labor Day"
The Wilderness House Literary Review; "Hershey Gardens"
Bluepepper; "The Path to Citizenship" Foliate Literary
Magazine; "Crickets" Foliate Literary Magazine; "Cornucopia"
Bluepepper; "At the Cemetery" Millers Pond; "An Interloper"

"The earth was all before me. With a heart
Joyous, nor scared at its own liberty,
I look about; and should the chosen guide
Be nothing better than a wandering cloud,
I cannot miss my way."

— *William Wordsworth, The Prelude*

Contents:

*To my wife Theresa, who afforded me
countless hours alone.*

4th Of July

There are explosions in the distance;
I imagine it's what Egypt
must sound like, or Syria
to an extreme degree.
We face-paint the black sky
in old Chinese calligraphy,
holding our babies,
nearer to the previous generation
than any other, remembering
where we were when we first
heard Jimi Hendrix's rendition
of The Star Spangled Banner
and the casual aplomb
with which it was dismissed
over the snap of a
cheap pack of firecrackers.

5:00 PM

The moon,
like the silver head
of a thumbtack
pressed into
a blue sky—
as though someone
removed the note
about the stars.

8 rue Dupuytren

I'm thinking of Ernest Hemingway,
the way he may have arrived
at naming his book, 'The Sun Also Rises.'
He's sitting in a French cafe
and the aperitif he's ordered
is the last in the bottle,
thinking it's free,
as is the custom of American barkeeps.
He orders another.
The waiter brings it
along with the bill.
It wasn't free.
He has a word with the waiter
who's incredulous because
he knows of the author's fame,
and Hemingway explains "courtesy"
to a young man who never intended
for him to pay the bill
but simply autograph it
with the title
of his next book.

19 Degrees

It waits at the door,
not bowing inward
or loosening a hinge,
a purple rapture
whose very crescendo
is met turning the knob
and stepping into
its cantilevered lungs.

1964

The song came through
the mentholated smoke
of her cigarette,
in bits and hums.
Then a prepositional phrase
of some lover's plaint,
always followed
by a drag
and a sip of Pepsi
as she finished
the ironing
in the kitchen,
cooing
like a dove.

The Prognosis

Firewood, like bones,
femur, clavicle, rib.
The anatomy of October
spread against the sun
whose x-rays remain impenetrable.
Winter is in the marrow,
bones do not lie.

A Backyard Treatise

The ridge,
like a tsunami
in pluvious green,
rises above a
slouched clothesline
as though it were
Goliath against David.
And the lone clothespin,
the stone
in the slingshot.

A Baptismal Drive-Thru

Water falls rhythmically
from a severed rainspout
as if the church,
even in disrepair,
offers the water
of its neglect
to anyone willing
to stand under it
and imagine themselves
baptized.

Where the Pumpkins Grew

I'm staring out
at a bush
across my yard
jeweled in frost,
a misanthrope,
whose origins,
unlike Cinderella's carriage,
enjoy a generous curfew.

Wait

The sun rises,
carrying promise
in a golden basket,
she'll spread it out
on the picnic table
to which I run
with a bottle of wine
before she leaves.

A Beaut

He built a treehouse
high in a bony pine,
I mean way up.
He doesn't even
have any children.
It's a beauty though.
Other than killing
the tree with nails,
it's a beauty.

A Blissful Dichotomy

Surreptitiously, the bangles
of orange daylilies
and blue chicory
are left in the jewelry box.
The fields, transitioning
like a young woman
into her older years,
and the preference
for Queen Anne's Lace
as dignity supplants desire
the way summer
gives way to Autumn.

A Call

It was a voice
on the phone
I'd not heard
in nearly forty years,
since we were
childhood friends,
and it came to me
with the reverie
of really being related
to a Nigerian princess,
my good fortune
was only now beginning.

A Carnal Thought

The smell of summer
isn't hotdogs,
convertibles or fireworks.
It's the slender pistil
of a geranium
between your fingers,
her hairy hormones
secrete that sort of lust
that may have
abandoned you.

Dusk

One cloud
absorbs all
that is left
of the sun,
like old gauze
on a deepening bruise.

A Conflagration

The varietal birds
at the feeder
seem to acquiesce
to each other
until the cardinal,
his red plumage
like a Phoenix,
routs all observations.

A Dissolution

The day arrives
in monochrome,
filling the window
with a tirade
about this being
the day of your reckoning,
or as it has been said;
'The day you shall rue.'
So it is.
You sign the papers.
Was that two T's or two L's?
You pass a vase of flowers
on the receptionist's desk,
pluck a red carnation,
thread it into the buttonhole
of your jacket,
flaunting it
as you hurry
to your car.

A Distant Man

My grandfather
always walked
alone.
When he got
up for supper
or to return
to his chair—
to the bathroom,
of course,
and when
he retrieved
his newspaper
from the stoop.
He ascended
the steps
at night,
firmly gripping
his hand
along the banister,
and in the
long, dark hallway.
The cold linoleum
creaked
under his weight.

A Gala Evening

Couples approach the hotel
for some significant gathering,
all, very well dressed
so it must be a dignified affair.
There's distance between some,
a disagreement on the ride over,
maybe a state of separation?
Others, hand-in-hand,
conversing with each other.
Then, a pair, her arm
resting like a swan's neck
in the crook of his gentleness
the way words are softened
to the moment.

A Good Day to Stay In Bed

The remaining leaves
like shrapnel embedded
in the grey sky
that lumbers along,
crutched on earth,
sad unto death.

A Harbinger

The first summer
I hadn't gone swimming;
at fifty-nine-years-old.
The thought occurred to me,
the way a baby might
first see images, or
a relic uncovered
at an archaeological dig,
blowing the dust away reverently—
discovering truth
as it was known.

A Hummingbird

You can hear
their motor running
before you see them,
like a plane
passing above the clouds,
or that feeling
that comes with a prayer,
a tiny motor started,
nearly as invisible,
carried aloft,
dripping with nectar.

A January Night

The house is quiet
but for the jangling
of tags around
the dog's neck,
like the Ghost
of Christmas Past,
she shames me
into rubbing her belly.

A Man

He said,
"I look like
a POW, naked."
I looked at him
slumped in his chair.
The chemo had
singed the hair
on his head
and left only
corkscrew casings
of once vibrant conduit.
He was being
outsourced,
until the last
copper grommet
is removed
from the furnace
and the gauges
are unscrewed carefully
so as not
to break the glass.

A Memory

My grandmother's phone book
might as well be
an ancient scroll—
the numbers and exchanges
belong to the dead.
Written the way they were,
as if scribing
for a Pharaoh.
Once, my mother
jotted in the number
of a pizza shop,
and I retraced over
her galloping script,
knowing she'd have been
the only one to have
ever made that call.

A Nod to Richard Brautigan

The crane is tilted
over the trees
as though it were
a giant fishing pole
and the cars going by
are disinterested fish,
but a few slow down
to watch it hoist
a transformer of sorts,
lured by the trapeze
of so unlikely a catch.

A Nor'easter

The wind moves about,
slathering the branches,
summoning the clouds
to announce further sanctions,
but the snow
has congealed into a crust.
The wind moves on,
colder, angrier than ever.

Home

Evening settles
like a soft comb
through mahogany hair,
the clatter of supper dishes
stacked one on top
of the other
still warm
from the dishwater,
love and weariness
crenellated into this
clapboard fortress.

A Photograph

Looking outside
the window,
this morning
the tone is sepia,
the trees and
surrounding brush
like immigrants
staring back, sternly.

A Physician's Lament

Outside the doctor's office
trucks and cars clot the road
while inside they form
a line at the sliding board,
their glee, the pressure
rising in veins.

A Place in the Shade

"We should have
a nice pitcher
with matching glasses,"
you said.
You'll make lemonade
for when
Nancy, from the
Jehovah Witnesses,
comes over.
We'll sit out
on the front porch.
She'll puzzle again
over the Trinity,
and we'll
look at each other,
then back at Nancy.
We'll raise
the lemonade
to our lips
and try
to remember
what the
question was.

A Reader

What is a home to
a twenty-seven-year-old?
An apartment?
A berth in the belly
of a battleship?
Or maybe the easy confines
among an uninspiring job,
faithful friends, and cheap beer.
All, but for an exception
noted today,
a wily footnote
rising from the bottom
of the page:
Nodule.
Maybe seven or eight
on the lungs.
Home, suddenly, is sacrosanct.
The page bookmarked.

A Road-Show

The wind rolls in
like a card dealer
whose credentials were
suspended in Kansas City.
He gathers all
around the table,
explains the rules
in Celsius,
deals the cards,
then raises the ante.

A Rudimentary Explanation

I wonder if Galileo,
having pronounced
earth revolves
around the sun,
may have used
a robin's egg
and a dandelion
to demonstrate it
for the Pope.

A Small Bang Theory

The partial shell
of a robin's egg
lies on the ground,
its blueness like earth
in a sea of green,
a vast yard of
tightly cropped grass
where this tiny fragment
has begun its universe.

Wildflowers

A pod of intransigence
has picketed my yard,
yellow bangles
clumped together
like striking factory workers
mooning a sun
that caves to their demands.

A Street of Love

While harried parents
grab their hands
and usher them along,
children marvel
at a puddle
of water
in the perfect shape
of a heart.

A TKO?

The wind boxed
with a treetop
until the tree
got the upper hand
and sent the wind
sailing to the canvass
with a relentless series
of leafy jabs.
The wind regrouped
on a clothesline,
snapping sheets
like a corner-man
waving smelling salts.

A Veteran's Reunion

His hair is white, wavy
the way smoke moves
on a still night.
He punctuates his stride
in acquiescence to thought,
his forearms a burl
of tattoos turned magenta.
He studies the lanyard,
the flag sagging.
The concierge is talking
to a young lady.
He remembers a girl in France
gathering eggs barefoot,
her lips fatted
preternaturally red,
the sunken color
of his morbidity,
the bus motor thrumming.

A Winter's Redaction

The ash of Hiroshima,
this snow incinerated-white,
as though this house
were by a crematory.
Only the darling tracks
of so many birds
make it not so.

A Writ

The grasses
behind the barn
are nearly white,
whiskery-grey,
as the sun
slouches away
like a constable
having served notice.

A Wynken, Blynken and Nod Moment

When I woke this morning
there was white everywhere,
as if the moon had spilt, or,
having not been secured
to the night sky, fell,
and shattered to pieces
like a china plate.

A Deciduous Reckoning

After the first frost,
leaves take such
divergent paths
to the ground,
like tiny lifeboats
fleeing their ships
for the silvery unknown.

Abscond

The trees rise
to the sudden sun,
as if awakened
from a nap,
to be cloaked
in gold,
only to have it
taken from them
the way their
silver cummerbunds
are removed
in the morning.

Across The Knob

The crocuses flicker,
blue flames,
a pod of pilot lights
where nary a recipe
abandons its blooms,
and the finger scalded
is the first to be kissed.

After October

The trees are naked infantrymen
stripped of dignity,
horded in a gulag,
no medical care
for the squirrel nests
that have metastasized
into tumors.

After the Season

While cleaning out
a bluebird box
I came across
two perfectly
skeletonized babies,
nestled in hardened
moss and twigs—
their delicate craniums
facing each other.

Aging
-45 years ago

10:00 AM on
a Saturday morning,
my brother and I
would be knocking
on our
Friend's doors,
To get a
Box-ball game going
at 59th & Greenway Avenue.
Now,
my brother is dead
and I watch the cardinals
and bluebirds
at the birdfeeder.
A redheaded woodpecker
has his fidgety talons
in the suet cake
a thousand miles
from there.

A Reason for Purgatory

Burlap with
the verisimilitude
of sackcloth.
A daily communicant
grieving through Mass,
a pogrom of ruby flies
droning their dirge
of a mendicant soul.

All Things Alive

I wonder, after
having cut down
a tree in front
of my house
and burning a piece
the next morning
in the woodstove,
if it smells
to the woods
like Auschwitz did
to the Jews,
on those cold,
grey days.

All Things Relative

The willow tree
leans over
pilloried in frost
the way Lot's wife
was in salt.
And once again,
through the eye
of a witness,
all truth
comes to pass.

Alleluia

The snow comes down
like so much confetti,
but all white,
as if the gates of heaven
have jarred loose,
releasing all these pretty souls
for us to love again.

Along Erly Road

A derelict apple tree
invites the melancholia
of forgotten entreaties,
on the ashen bark
an initial in a stanchion of sap,
like that first kiss,
still pollinating itself
against all odds.

Along the Road

Globules of honey
in glass jars
on a porch
for sale,
together with grasshoppers
sustained John the Baptizer.

Cornucopia

The bees, fatted
on the goldenrod,
like Chinese junks
in a typhoon,
sinking into
a yellow sea.

Crickets

Early Autumn
a lowing from
Jack-in-the-pulpit's
invisible music,
almost tinnitus
on sheets of dawn.

Alphabet

Letters have fallen overnight
into my yard.
At first glance
it looks like a mass grave
with L's, R's, F's upturned,
B's pell-mell,
the crush of D's and Q's
atop the pile,
even Z's unceremoniously dumped.
Zeus would not be pleased.

Amenity

The cat thinks
I'm his doorman—
up, down,
in, out.
As if this
were the Dorchester
and I
the paid help.

American Countryside

I saw Claude Monet
in Mannsville;
his terse poignant-orange,
dappling a purple paste
in concentric swirls,
gracefully adjudicating
the peace of light
across a licorice pigment
chosen for the pond.

American L'Astrance

My wife and I stopped
for dinner at McDonald's.
She took a table
in a sunny nook
while I brought
our order over
and bowed
to a lovely acquisition
that was ours
for the moment.

A 6:00 AM Appointment

The blue jays rearrange
themselves on the tree,
musicians vying for a part,
trilling collectively
their sameness,
the audition concludes
without surprise.

Choreography

Dawn opens groggily,
strafed by barren limbs,
reeling, it seems, from
a disconcerting evening
where the stars
in their ambivalence
shook themselves
from a thousand years
of steadiness and smote
the way embers do
before the rain,
the philosophy of survival.

An End

A groundhog squats
in the garden,
pawing at frost,
making a paste
like Jesus did.
Only for nothing.
The rust gathers
in the fields
and the trees
come to a halt, naked,
lifting the moon
in their emaciated fingers
away from this famine.

An Engineer's Muse

The geese sound
from above the cloud cover.
I imagine them flying
in the perfected 'V' formation.
I'm wondering if they'll
descend within my view,
that I might better understand
the aerodynamics
of the new 787 Dreamliner,
or, if they'll continue on,
leaving me to extrapolate
a glitch or two.

An Interloper

In the quiet
before the first snow,
the fire crackles
in the woodstove,
the cat pensive
above the chair,
both of us staring
into the gray air.
A woodpecker lands
on the suet cake,
and for a moment
we are plucked
from our fixation,
like dreamers
awakened by a kiss.

An Old Saw

The crickets,
like so many
summery volcanoes,
incline towards the
dormancy of frost
in that magma
of red grasses
and hardened earth.

An Old Woman in Church

Her arms,
like blanched asparagus,
rested on the pew.
A lanyard of glossy
black-oracles
unraveled from
her fingertips.
She raised them
and kissed
the Crucifix,
letting it fall
from her lips
in tiny peals
of utter despair—
clacking, clacking,
clacking.

Annihilation

The torturous truth
remains torturous,
spoken from quadrants
together, piecemeal.
Perhaps, canon to canon,
fuses lit,
in a moment
a million atoms
explode into new obfuscation.

Anniversary

The unwinding of years,
as though it were a bale
of scraps, pieces, threads,
something in back
of the junk drawer.
Death, thin as a bread-tie,
not the least bit dazzling,
as the lace from a prom shoe
severed in mid-stride
by a girl who moves
across the floor
the way longing
bungles a heart
into love.

Antithesis

Christmas is a sort
of rumination
on whether a heart,
in some inexplicable sentiment,
succumbs to its enormity
to that promise
separated by separation.

Art

On a rainy day
in September,
behind a school bus,
the windshield
becomes a canvass
running with yellow,
red, crimson paint-splotches,
if only between
intermittent wipers,
wet and splattered
as if thrown
from a bucket
Jackson Pollock style.

As Days Go By

Daylilies like paparazzi
peer over the fence
on elongated stems
in the stanched silence
of soft, orange flashes.

The Ramp

A ramp is
the first sign
of a home
in distress.
Like cancer,
it changes
everything.
Oh, the neighbors
will say
it's barely noticeable,
a flower here,
a shrub there,
when deep down,
like you,
they're devastated.
They try
to imagine it
on their house
but the thought
of tearing out
the rhododendrons
is worse.

As Time Goes By

My brother rims
a vast complexity
of narrowing conflictions,
those in the forefront
of my mind,
along the labyrinth,
retreating to those
in the rear,
as though failing
to get into
the Baseball Hall of Fame,
become daguerreotypes
of the vanquished.

For Sale

A magnolia distributes
pink communion wafers
that fall, lamentably,
beneath a gaping tessitura
of windows, their dirge
like the apples
left in the barn
are all this farmhouse
can herald.

At an Intersection

A slogan in
block letters
on the truck,
"Eat More Bananas"
above the cursive
"Bananas Our Specialty."
I wonder if,
opening the door,
I might find him,
the driver, working
among great fronds,
emerald green snakes.
Maybe a silverback gorilla
deep in the corner,
waiting.

At Ease

Dahlia's fall out
of formation,
filling with orange,
drowsy, the way
soldiers learn
hurry up and wait.

At the Car Show

He was old,
stooping as
best he could,
to dab protectant
on to the
Redline tires
of his '63 Corvette.
"Do ya' ever
Drive it?"
"Yup!"
And I tried
to imagine
his grey hair,
almond bronze,
top down
and the wind
pursing the
sculpted red-lips
of a girl
riding shotgun.

At the Cemetery

January is such
a conducive month
to die.
It's cold and dark.
The trees are blank,
and that uncle
who's cheating
on his wife
invariably arrives late
to a chorus
of vapory exhalations.

With a Nod to Shel Silverstein

If I could flip my lawn,
suspend it in the air,
the stems of dandelions
would look like nose-hair.

Dix Hill Farm

The sky heals itself
as though it were a wound
inflicted by relentless lightening
whose varicose veins
collapse into a rouge
of sienna and cream
as sheep bleat
and rouse the cradle cap
from their fleece.

Kittyhawk

A disheveled Monarch butterfly
Lay dead in the grass,
Its papery wings
Separated in flight
Like orange thrusters
Still glowing
After the crash.

Lovers

A leaf falls,
were it a dream
detached from the dreamer,
a scarlet key
to whose locket
with the same initials
as is carved
into its trunk.

Kissed by God at Ski Roundtop

It came gradually
as it might be
expected to do.
The trees, Peruvian green
rise up the slope,
instead of a burning bush,
an agave blue sky
penitent with clouds
and the burdock of chance.

From the Duncannon Train Trestle

A cloud has landed belly-up
on the Susquehanna river
like Sully Sullenberger
touching down on the Hudson.
But this flight is pilotless,
there aren't any passengers
to stand on the wings.
Just a nimbus
strayed from the pod
enveloping a fisherman
casting a line
into its empty fuselage.

Defeat at Little Buffalo Park

Trees thin to
bony appendages,
scarlet blood
in fallen leaves.
And the sky
hurls blue spears
in glorious arcs.

Plumage

The barn wrested
as much sun
was available.
Planks sunburned,
the cinnamon rim
of a basketball hoop
like an earring.
Corn, gold as broom thistle
where the hinges
run like mascara.

Labor Day

Water in the pool
is murky, still.
The pump off.
Marigold petals flitter
beneath the surface as Koi.
A diving board
splays the end
where once she cleaved
to her freshly risen breasts,
gone, but for clods of grapes
basking, as is their way
in slanted light.

1963 Redux

Cicadas are chatty tonight
as if the trees were
Brooklyn tenements
and everyone's TV
was tuned to
Walter Cronkite's report
that the young president was dead,
that the wash strung
between the buildings
would stay there until
the last sob is quieted.

Hershey Gardens

Evening is formal,
the setting sun
a tangerine light
through shadows
in dark tuxedos,
her green musicality,
they primp and fawn
hand in hand for pictures
as he gently hoops a ring from Saturn,
the rosy one,
over her moonlet wrist.

Frost Warning

I'm thinking of
the word, isotope.
But not in the sense
of the cold war.
More, the peach petals
on a timeline,
and none too soon
for me to step out
into the moonlight
and breathe in
a Florentine fresco
iced in silver.

Spring Cantata

The day begins
a fledgling symphony
then the score
is rearranged by wind,
a Treble Clef is flattened
by the slog of a turtle.
Peepers, in superfluous half-beats
usurped by hooves
that sink into
a baritone of mud
and a trilling
is the hook
as a requiem of clouds
portend the curtain.

Weekend Warrior

It was our first
riding lawnmower.
The opulence.
A Sears Craftsman,
silver with honeycomb headlights
and a brutish crawl
like a halftrack
in Rommel's panzer division.

The House

They say the place was left.
A coterie of vines
with orange knuckles
grips the rain gutter,
a lilac bush crams
its purple-faced commuters
between the spindles
of the porch railing.
Cattails sound
from the pond
a brown suede xylophone.
And a mattress spring
is scrimshawed onto
the white-washed bones
of the barn.

Hershey Lodge

There are blossoms
strewn across the chair
where you were sitting
last night talking to me
and now, lovely reminders
of your sentences reincarnated.

A Recusal

The first frost,
a gossamer snow
where grass and leaves
are gathered
into a festive reunion,
the dead are remembered
bigger than life
until the sun rises
and the last
blade of grass
returns its silvery tuxedo
the way my father
was reluctant
to give my mother up
after their dance.

Laundry Day

The clouds are
full of tarnish
after buffing
the moon all night
and in the morning
their collection has begun,
siphoning into a creek,
thickening the water
where stones agitate
them clean.

A Collaboration

There's a statue
of the Blessed Virgin Mary
on the kitchen sink
next to a soap dispenser.
Her arms are open, the way
She is usually depicted
and in this place
She's exuding bubbles
that rise to her plastic feet
through the intersession of one
fumbling to open the drain.

The Path to Citizenship

You can almost hear the fife and drum.
What are the Federalist Papers?
How many amendments are there
to the Constitution?
A couple speak to each other
in Guatemalan.
On this day, a celebrity judge
will do the oath.
He's affable, tall with shiny hair.
He tells a joke, people look for a snare.
A woman clerk sets aside an Edwardian novel
and passes around miniature American flags.
After The Pledge of Allegiance
there are pictures, light snacks.
An old man wearing a necklace of bones
contemplates a portrait of Ronald Reagan,
in particular, a white handerkerchief
in his left breast pocket, monogrammed
the way the man's bones are known to him.

November Elegy

The patio;
a pail of rain
lumpy with leaves
and a sky, moribund,
in the bony fingers
of trees.

Arlene's Barn

Its trapezoid bones,
the constellations
in board feet.
An Aurora Borealis
of paint swatches.
The blue bulb
of a lightening rod
like bottled anger.

Thanksgiving

October tarnishes into November.
The sky, flatware
set out after the last
of the black walnuts
has been run over on the road
and the good dishes
retrieved from the cupboard.

November

Its a graveyard-looking
sort of day
with all of the dead leaves
as though there'd been
a massacre
and the sky
as a backhand
across the face
as the skeletal remains
of the trees trudge home
with only their shadows
to guide them.

Autism Tree

The bark is of good stock,
limbs as they should be,
but the sap, maquillage
on so many crooked faces,
the way Vermeer saw Delft
in Lupis-lazuli and Indian yellow.

42514291R00070

Made in the USA
Charleston, SC
31 May 2015